EXPLORE AUSTRALIA
12 KEY FACTS

by Todd Kortemeier

12 STORY LIBRARY

www.12StoryLibrary.com

12-Story Library is an imprint of Bookstaves.

Photographs ©: lovleah/iStockphoto, cover, 1; David Nicolson/CC4.0, 4; Richard Ling/CC3.0, 5; Nick Pitsas/CSIRO, 6; David Clode/Unsplash, 7; Library of Congress, 8; Victoria Jones/Pool PA/Associated Press, 10; katacarix/Shutterstock.com, 11; STRINGERimage/iStockphoto, 12; ThitareeSarmkasat/iStockphoto, 13; sirtravelalot/Shutterstock.com, 14; Ann Hodgson/Shutterstock.com, 15; NASA, 16; NASA, 17; Matthew Kane/Unsplash, 18; Evad37/CC3.0, 19; Ilia Torlin/Shutterstock.com, 20; olaser/iStockphoto, 21; Steve Evans/CC2.0, 22; Blulz60/iStockphoto, 23; Nils Versemann/Shutterstock.com, 24; davidf/iStockphoto, 25; xavierarnau/iStockphoto, 26; amophoto_au/Shutterstock.com, 27; Globe Turner/Shutterstock.com, 28; Nannucci/iStockphoto, 29

ISBN
978-1-63235-550-8 (hardcover)
978-1-63235-667-3 (hosted ebook)

Library of Congress Control Number: 2018937840

Printed in the United States of America
Mankato, MN
June 2018

About the Cover
Australia's famous Sydney Opera House
and Sydney Harbour Bridge at dusk.

Access free, up-to-date content on this topic plus a full digital version of this book. Scan the QR code on page 31 or use your school's login at 12StoryLibrary.com.

Table of Contents

Australia Is the Island Continent

Australia is both a country and a continent. It is sometimes referred to as the island continent. But Australia is actually made up of many islands. There are more than 8,000 of them. The mainland is the biggest of these islands. Tasmania is the next largest.

In total, Australia is nearly three million square miles (7.7 million sq km) in size. That makes it the sixth-largest country by area on Earth. As a large nation, Australia has many different landscapes. Over one-third of Australia receives so little rain that it is effectively desert. This includes the famous outback. The region is hot and dry with almost no plants. But Australia also has lush rainforests and snow-capped mountains.

Most Australians live in the southwest and southeast. These areas are cooler and more comfortable than most northern regions. Australia's six most populated cities are on the coastline.

Uluru, formerly known as Ayers Rock, is a rock formation that originally sat at the bottom of a sea 600 million years ago.

16,007
**Miles of coastline
(25,760 km) of the
Australian mainland.**

- Australia is a huge
  country with many
  different landscapes.
- More than one-third of
  Australia is made up of
  desert.
- Most cities are located in
  the cooler southwest and
  southeast.
- Australia also has
  tall mountains and
  underwater coral reefs.

A blue starfish
on the Great
Barrier Reef.

PERTH,
THE LONELY CITY

In Australia, most cities are
scattered around the coasts.
And these are mainly on
the eastern side, including
Sydney. But Perth is located
on the western side of the
island. The city is 2,045 miles
(3,291 km) from Sydney.
Perth is the most isolated
major city in the world.

Some parts of Australia are
mountainous. The largest mountain
range is the Great Dividing Range.
Mount Kosciuszko is its highest
peak. It stands 7,310 feet (2,228 m)
high. The Australian coast is home
to many coral reefs. The largest of
these is the Great Barrier Reef. It is
the largest coral reef in the world,
stretching over 1,800 miles (3,000
km) off the northeastern coast.

Different Climates Led to Biological Diversity

There is no single climate in Australia. The country is huge. Climate depends heavily on location.

In the center of the country is the outback. Conditions are very hot and dry. Some areas may not receive rain for years. At the other extreme, the northeast coast can be very rainy. Snow is rare in most parts of the country. It can mostly be seen on the highest mountain peaks. Southern areas of Australia are most comfortable.

Bushfires are common in Australia. Drought can make them more likely. In 2009, the Black Saturday fires killed 173 people. It was the biggest loss of life due to fire in the country's history. In wet seasons, dry regions may be impacted by dangerous flash floods. Australia's coasts are also at risk of cyclones.

Varying climates make Australia one of the most biologically diverse countries. More than one million species of plants and animals live in different habitats across Australia. Less than half have ever been scientifically studied.

Eighty-four percent of Australia's mammals are found only on the continent. Two famous examples are also marsupials: the kangaroo and koala. Australia has more than 140 species of marsupials.

Kinglake National Park after the Black Saturday bushfires.

Koalas mainly eat eucalyptus leaves.

DANGEROUS CREATURES

Some of Australia's many creatures are deadly. More poisonous snakes live in the country than anywhere else. The inland taipan is the world's most venomous snake. Australia also has deadly insects, fish, and spiders. The European honey bee is the deadliest of all. Its sting can cause a fatal allergic reaction in some people.

4,000
Species of fish in Australia's waters.

- Australia has many different climates.
- Bushfires and cyclones are natural disasters that affect Australia.
- Australia is one of the world's most biologically diverse countries.
- Most of Australia's mammals are unique to the country.

Europeans Displaced Indigenous Peoples

As a country, Australia is not that old. It has existed for just over a century. But people have lived on the island for 50,000 years. These native people are called Aboriginal Australians. Aboriginal society evolved into various clans. These groups lived off the land. They hunted and fished game to survive. Nobody else set foot on the island until 1606.

Willem Janszoon was the first European to land in Australia. He and his crew mapped about 186 miles (300 km) of coastline. Australia was a major discovery for the Europeans. People had long believed there was another continent on Earth. It was called *Terra Australis Incognita* in Latin. The name meant "unknown southern land."

Many other explorers soon followed. James Cook arrived in 1770. He claimed Australia for Great Britain. European settlers brought disease.

A camp of aborigines in North Queensland in 1921.

The Aborigines had never had contact with any other people. They could not fight off new germs. Many people died. There also was war. Aborigines fought back as their land was taken by Europeans.

The first European colony was New South Wales. It was formed in 1788. The colony was used as a prison for British criminals. That era ended when a British government was established in 1823. British influence spread and new states were formed. In 1901, Australia became an independent nation.

54
Number of European ships that visited Australia between 1606 and 1770.

- Aborigines have lived in Australia for 50,000 years.
- The first European explorer arrived in 1606.
- Disease and war killed many Aboriginal people.
- Australia became its own country in 1901.

TIMELINE

50,000 BCE: First record of humans in Australia.

1606: Dutch explorer William Janszoon is the first European to land on the continent.

1770: James Cook arrives and claims Australia for Great Britain.

1901: Australia becomes an independent country.

1911: Canberra is named the nation's capital.

1986: The Australian constitution severs all ties to the British legal system.

4

The Government Is a Constitutional Monarchy

Australia became an independent nation in 1901. But it still has some ties to the United Kingdom. Queen Elizabeth II rules over both the UK and Australia. But the British government does not control Australia.

Queen Elizabeth is the head of state. She has no role in running the government. She rarely even visits the country. Instead, she appoints a Governor-General. He or she serves in Australia for her.

The Australian prime minister is the head of government. This person is the leader of the largest party in the House of Representatives. The house is one of two bodies that make up Australia's legislature. The other is the Senate. Together, these two houses are known as Parliament. They make the laws in Australia. The law of the land is the

Queen Elizabeth II meets with Prime Minister Malcolm Turnbull at Buckingham Palace in London.

Australia's Federation Guard is a ceremonial unit within the Department of Defence.

Constitution of Australia. The High Court is in charge of interpreting the constitution. It determines how laws are applied.

Australia's military is called the Australian Defence Force (ADF). It has three services. They are the Royal Australian Navy, Australian Army, and Royal Australian Air Force. Australians are active members. Serving is not required for citizens.

29

Number of Australian prime ministers up to and including Malcolm Turnbull (2015–).

- Australia is independent but has ties to the UK.
- Queen Elizabeth II is Queen of Australia but has little official role.
- The prime minister leads Parliament as head of government.
- The Australian Defence Force is the country's military.

5
Australia's Economy Is Thriving

Australia is one of the richest countries in its part of the world. One way to measure an economy is by GDP. It stands for gross domestic product. GDP is the total value of all goods a country produces. Australia's GDP was $1.2 trillion in 2016. That ranks 14th in the world.

Many of Australia's exports are natural resources. Iron ore is the largest. It makes up 24 percent of all exports. Next are coal (17 percent) and gold (8 percent). Australia also exports manufactured goods such as cars and electronics.

Australia imports a lot of items, too. Cars make up 9 percent of Australia's imports. That is the largest category. Gasoline is next at 6 percent, then computers at 3 percent. Because of its location, Australia mostly trades with Asian countries. China is its biggest trading partner. Japan and South Korea are also important partners.

An iron ore pit in Western Australia.

AUSSIE CURRENCY

The currency of Australia is the Australian dollar. Bills come in denominations of $5, $10, $20, $50, and $100. Coins come in denominations of 5, 10, 20 and 50 cents as well as one and two dollars. Dollar bills pay tribute to many great Australians. The $50 bill features David Unaipon, an Aboriginal writer and inventor. Coins depict symbols of Australia. Dollar coins feature five kangaroos. Queen Elizabeth II is also featured on a few designs.

$159 billion

Australia's total exports in 2016.

- Australia has one of the strongest economies in its region.
- Most exports are natural resources.
- Most imports are manufactured products.
- Australia's biggest trading partners are in Asia.

Australian currency is the first to be printed on polymer (plastic).

All Children Receive an Education

Kids in Australia start school when they are five or six. Some schooling is required for everybody. Each state determines how much. Children typically must go to school until they are 15 or 16. The Australian school year runs from January to December. Classes are taught in the national language of English. Students study in eight key learning areas. Among them are math, science, and art.

Students who want to pursue higher education have two choices. One track is Vocational Education and Training (VET). VET programs prepare students for a specific career. The other option is to go to a university. Universities offer a wide range of degrees.

VET programs are usually focused on one type of job. Students graduate with a certificate.

Science is a key learning area for students in Australia.

Students attend Open Day at the University of Sydney to learn about campus life.

The document shows they are qualified to do a job. VET programs offer training for many industries.

Automotive and construction are two examples.

Students who go to a university study broader topics. This education is a little more general. Students can get a wide range of jobs with a university degree. But it is more expensive. Tuition often costs tens of thousands of dollars per year.

There are 43 universities in Australia. More than a million students attend each year. The University of Sydney is the oldest. It was founded in 1850. It ranks among the world's best institutions for higher education.

Australia Is Strong in Science and Technology

Australia is a science and technology leader in its region. The country has a long history of success in these fields. Twelve Australians have won the Nobel Prize in scientific

spend billions of dollars each year on scientific research. Businesses and nonprofit organizations are also responsible for advances in the sciences.

Andy Thomas took his first flight into space aboard the US space shuttle *Endeavour.*

Australia has made several major contributions to space exploration. A communications station in Canberra helped land the *Curiosity* rover on Mars in 2012. The same station also helped relay images of Pluto in 2015. Andy Thomas became Australia's first professional astronaut in 1995.

Australia is a leader in mining. The land is rich in resources. Iron ore, coal, and gold are some of the most heavily mined materials. A relatively new focus of mining is on technology metals. These are materials used to make computers and other

The first signals from NASA's *Curiosity* rover as it landed on Mars were sent to Australia.

electronic devices. They are likely to be a source of growth in Australia's economy for years to come.

2.3 million

Number of Australians qualified to work in science, technology, engineering, and mathematics fields.

- Australia is a science leader in its part of the world.
- It has a long history of scientific exploration.
- Australia has made major contributions to space exploration.

THINK ABOUT IT

What scientific achievements have been made in your home country? Who are some people responsible for important advances in science, technology, engineering, and mathematics? Read and research online to find answers.

The Infrastructure Offers Many Ways to Get Around

The highway along Sydney's Royal National Park.

10

Percent of Australia's GDP spent on infrastructure in 2016.

- Australia has an extensive system of roads.
- Highway 1 goes all the way around the country.
- People also use buses and trains to get around.
- Air travel links Australia with the rest of the world.

AUSTRALIANS LOVE CARS

In 2017, there were 18.8 million cars registered in Australia. The population of Australia was 24.5 million. That means about three-quarters of all Australians own cars. The country has one of the world's highest rates of car ownership. Only one in 10 Australians uses public transportation to get to work.

Because Australia is such a large country, cars are important for travel. The country has a well-established system of roadways. There are more than 500,000 miles (804,672 km) of streets and highways. That is the ninth-most in the world. People in Australia drive on the left side of the road.

Australia is connected by national highways. They link most major cities. Highway 1 is Australia's most important highway. It goes all the way around the country. That is a journey of nearly 15,000 miles (24,140 km). More than a million people use Highway 1 each day.

People in major cities are less reliant on cars. Most have access to buses and trains. Cities on the coast often have ferry systems, too. Trains also link Australia's major cities. Most operate on the east coast. But the Indian Pacific takes passengers from Sydney to Perth in three days. Air travel is very important in Australia. As an island country, it is relatively isolated from the rest of the world. And its large size can make car or rail travel impractical.

Sydney Airport handles most visitors to Australia. It is one of the oldest continuously operating airports in the world. About 43 million people use it each year. Other major airports are located in Brisbane, Melbourne, and Perth. Perth has the only international airport in western Australia.

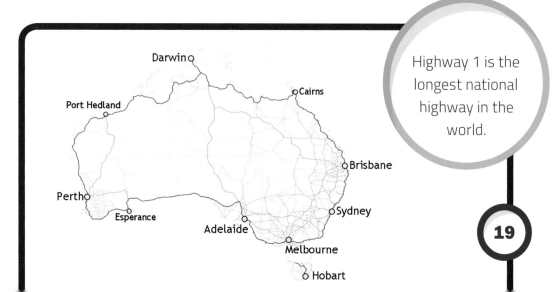

Highway 1 is the longest national highway in the world.

Most Australians Have British Ancestry

Australia is home to more than 24 million people. From 2015 to 2016, the population grew by nearly 400,000. Australia is a large country in terms of physical size, but not by population. It is not even in the top 50 worldwide.

Most Australians are descended from Europeans. The majority of these people were British. Aboriginal Australians make up about 3 percent of the population. Among this indigenous people are many different clans.

Before Europeans arrived, there were more than 500 clans. Each had its own culture and language. Aboriginal Australians today maintain their clan heritage and beliefs.

Australia has encouraged immigration since the mid-1900s. Most immigrants have come from Asia. They make up about 12 percent of the population. About half are Chinese-Australians. Immigration is part of Australia's emphasis on multiculturalism. It has been part of government policy since 1973.

It's believed some Aboriginal rock engravings date back 50,000 years.

7.9 million

Number of people in New South Wales, the most populous state in Australia.

- Australia has a population of more than 24 million people.
- Australia is multicultural, but most people are of British ancestry.
- Aboriginal Australians make up 3 percent of the population.
- Most immigrants arrive from Asia.

PLENTY OF SPACE

Australians have plenty of elbow room. The country is huge in size, with a relatively small population. It has a third as many people as the United Kingdom. And the UK is a much smaller island in terms of physical size. Australia averages 7.5 people per square mile (3.1 per sq km). That is seventh-lowest in population density in the world.

Sydney, in New South Wales, has the largest population in Australia.

Mandarin Chinese is the second-most spoken language. But less than 3 percent of the population speaks it. English is the national language. It is spoken by more than 70 percent of Australians.

Just over half of Australians are Christian. There are also small populations of Buddhists and Muslims. Nearly one-third of Australians claim no religion at all.

The Culture Is Uniquely Australian

Different groups of people contribute to Australia's overall culture. Aborigines have populated the land for 50,000 years. Their art, rituals, languages, and beliefs are still alive today. The didgeridoo is an Aboriginal musical instrument. It is one of Australia's most iconic symbols. Experts believe the wind instrument has been played by Aborigines for 40,000 years or longer.

An Aboriginal musician plays the didgeridoo.

Australians enjoy a wide range of foods. Many national dishes are influenced by Great Britain. Seafood is also very popular. Australia is surrounded by some of the freshest seafood anywhere. Some dishes are uniquely Australian. Vegemite is a thick, black food paste. Locals spread it on toast for almost any meal.

People in Australia celebrate most Christian holidays, including Easter and Christmas. Australia Day is the country's national holiday. Each January, it celebrates the arrival of British ships in 1788. Another unique national holiday is Anzac Day. It honors the first military action by Australia and New Zealand in World War I. The holiday takes place in April.

Aboriginal Australians have held festivals for thousands of years. They are sacred times for families to gather. The Garma Festival takes place in August. It is four days of dance, art, and traditional music.

THINK ABOUT IT

What are some of your favorite holidays, festivals, and other cultural activities? Are these events also popular with other people who live in your area?

20

Number of platinum-selling albums by AC/DC, the most by any Australian band.

- Many different groups of people contribute to Australian culture.
- Aboriginal traditions are important elements of the greater culture.
- Two important holidays are Australia Day and Anzac Day.
- Australians are passionate about sports, especially soccer.

Australians are also passionate about sports. Soccer is most popular. Australian rules football is a sport distinctive to the country. It is similar to rugby but has its own set of rules. Cricket and basketball are also popular.

Players compete for the ball in Australian rules football, which is similar to rugby.

23

Health Care Is Available to All Citizens

Australia provides health care to all citizens. The system is funded through taxes that people pay. The health care system doesn't just help the sick. It also focuses on preventing illness.

The Australian health care system is among the best in the world. This is a factor in Australians living an average of 82.3 years. That is 14th-highest in the world. Australia also has low infant and mother mortality rates. People are very healthy by most measures.

The cost of health care is low in Australia. Only 9.4 percent of GDP is spent on health care. That is 32nd-highest in the world. Many other countries spend more and have lower-quality care.

While Australia provides health care, it is not always easy for people to get it. This is especially true of those living in rural areas. People in these places generally receive lower-quality health care than city dwellers. They also experience higher rates of disease and premature death.

Some health problems are widespread in Australia. High blood pressure, arthritis, and high cholesterol are the most common

The Royal Melbourne Hospital is a major public teaching hospital.

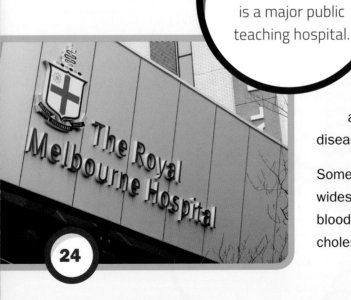

Schools have a strict no hat, no play policy for children.

conditions. These problems can be caused by obesity, which is also a concern.

Another major public health concern is skin cancer. Two in three Australians will get skin cancer by the age of 70. Harmful ultraviolet rays can be very strong in Australia. That doesn't stop people from spending a lot of time outdoors. Australia has one of the highest skin cancer rates in the world.

38.7
Median age in Australia, ranking 58th in the world.

- Australia provides health care to all citizens.
- Australia's health care system is highly ranked.
- It can be a challenge to provide high-quality care in rural areas.
- Skin cancer is a disease that affects many people.

12

The People Love Being Outdoors

Location is everything in Australia. Climate and lifestyle can vary greatly across different regions of the country.

THINK ABOUT IT

Do you live in a city or a rural area? What are some of the advantages of living where you live? What do you wish you could change about it?

Most Australians live a city lifestyle. Seventy-five percent of them live in the capital city of a state. Cities are well-developed with apartments, businesses, and office buildings. People enjoy access to public transportation. They have a wide range of jobs to choose from. People in rural areas, however, primarily work in farming, herding, or

Solar panels are on many homes in Australia.

mining. Houses and farms are more common there.

One thing is common among many Australians. They enjoy being outdoors as often as possible. Surfing is one of the most popular activities.

25,594
Number of bike commuters in Melbourne, the most of any Australian city.

- Daily life varies across the different parts of Australia.
- Most Australians live in cities.
- Australia has a high cost of living.
- Most energy comes from coal.

Australia can be an expensive place to live. It has one of the highest costs of living in the world. Where people live makes a big difference. Cities like Sydney are very expensive. But less populated areas can be more affordable. Australia has to import a lot of goods, which adds to their expense. Food and gasoline can be costly.

Most of the energy Australia uses comes from fossil fuels. A large majority comes from coal. But Australia is also a leader in clean energy. One reason is that it receives a great deal of sunlight. Solar power is increasingly harnessed to power the country. More than 1.5 million people have installed solar panels on their homes.

Australia at a Glance

Population in 2018: 24,598,900

Area: 2,969,907 square miles (7,692,024 sq km)

Capital: Canberra

Largest Cities: Sydney, Melbourne, Brisbane, Perth, Adelaide

Flag:

National Language: English

Currency: Australian Dollar

What people who live in Australia are called: Australians or Aussies

Where in the World?

Australia

Glossary

clan

Group of people who share common heritage and beliefs.

colony

Area of land claimed and settled by another country.

constitution

Document that is the law of the land in a country.

coral reef

Underwater area where coral lives.

cyclone

Type of storm with rotating winds that can cause great damage.

denominations

Amounts in which a country issues its money.

infrastructure

Basic structures and systems needed for a country to function, like roads, bridges, and communication systems.

legislature

Group or groups of people who make laws in a country.

mainland

Largest land area in a country.

marsupial

Mammal that carries its young in a pouch.

mortality rate

Rate at which people die.

ore

Raw form of certain metals.

rugby

Sport in which two teams try to score by advancing a ball.

For More Information

Books

Perritano, John. *Australia: Tradition, Culture, and Daily Life.* Broomall, PA: Mason Crest, 2016.

Gitlin, Marty. *Australia.* Country Profiles. Minneapolis, MN: Bellwether Media, 2018.

Owings, Lisa. *Learning about Australia.* Do You Know the Continents? Minneapolis, MN: Lerner Publishing Group, 2016.

Visit 12StoryLibrary.com

Scan the code or use your school's login at **12StoryLibrary.com** for recent updates about this topic and a full digital version of this book. Enjoy free access to:

- Digital ebook
- Breaking news updates
- Live content feeds
- Videos, interactive maps, and graphics
- Additional web resources

Note to educators: Visit 12StoryLibrary.com/register to sign up for free premium website access. Enjoy live content plus a full digital version of every 12-Story Library book you own for every student at your school.

Index

About the Author

Todd Kortemeier is a journalist and children's author from Minnesota. He has written more than 50 books for young people. He and his wife live in Minneapolis.

READ MORE FROM 12-STORY LIBRARY

Every 12-Story Library Book is available in many fomats. For more information, visit 12StoryLibrary.com

32